Raphael (1483-1520) **MADONNA OF THE CHAIR** Pitti Palace, Florence

Your Picture. This picture is your very own. Try to be very careful of it till Christmas time. Then you can put it on a calendar for mother. You must keep it as a big surprise. How safe the little Christ Child feels in His Mother's arms! See how close His Mother holds Him to her. Just like your mother would hold you. Would you like to be the little boy at her knee? He has been playing with the Baby Jesus. He was Our Lord's little cousin. He seems to know that the Baby is God. And he feels it is wonderful to be so close to Him. See his hands. They are like yours when you come close to God and talk to Him. The little cousin became St. John the Baptist. When you are bigger you will have another picture of St. John. Now your teacher will tell you a lovely story about this picture.

Your Name. When you were a tiny baby your Godparents carried you to church. The priest baptized you. He gave you your name and made you one of God's children. You were too little to talk so your Godparents told God for you that when you were bigger you would love Him. Long ago our dear Lord lived beside the sea. His friends caught fish. They were called fishermen. Our Lord baptized them. They were the first Christians. The wicked king hated Christians. When they wanted to tell a new friend about being baptized they would draw a fish. They did not want the wicked king to know what they said. Look at the picture and make your Baptism Name Book.

Fruit. Would you like to have a party? Let us play we are gathering the fruit from the trees for our party. Let us see which fruit looks like some other fruit. Can you cut it from paper? Now let us color it. Does it tell you its name when it is finished? We will end our party with a game. Mary will gather up all the fruit. Each row will choose a captain. We shall see which captain can name the most fruit. Do you thank God when you eat fruit? You know He sends the rain and sun to make it grow. Find pictures of fruit at home to paste on the blank page to help us know the color.

EAS

Trees. Let us play that the pencil is a train. The picture shows it on track number four. Each time it must start from the station at the bottom on the wide track. You can choose the place to turn off for a new track. The second picture shows how the tracks make branches. Find pictures at home of the many lovely trees God has made. Paste them on the blank page to help us to know many shapes.

Color. Once upon a time the whole world was like darkest night. Then God created the sun and made light. It was His gift to all the things He had created. He wished to make them beautiful with color so He hid away in each bright sunbeam three lovely colors: red, yellow, and blue. He told the sunbeams to carry the colors to everything in the world. The sunbeams were happy because God had given them this beautiful secret for their very own. And they danced with joy because God wanted them to help Him. They knew God's gift was so wonderful that the world would love Him for it. Ask your teacher to show you how to share the sunbeam's secret. See whether you can find it on the color page. Do you know what the colors are saying to you? Some day your teacher will tell you that secret too. God made your soul beautiful and bright like a sunbeam. He hid it away in your body. He wants you to keep it like that until He calls it back to Him.

Your Letters. Let us fold a strip of paper. Make the two short edges even. Now fold again. Open the paper and cut the four blocks apart. The white lines in the picture show the path for the scissors. As we cut each letter we must be sure to cut on the path. After we have cut our letter let us place it beside the picture of the letter to see if it is like it. See which letters must be folded before being cut.

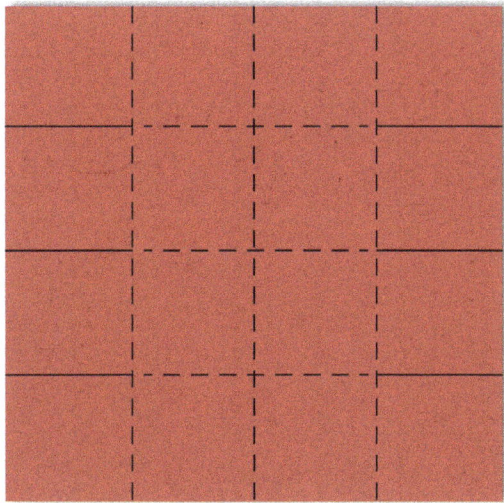

CUT ON SOLID LINES
PASTE TO FORM BODY OF CHURCH

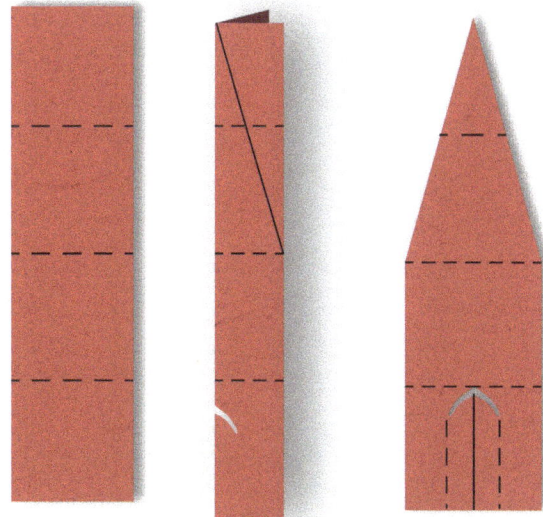

FOLD AND CUT FOR STEEPLE

FOLD—CUT 3 TREES AND PASTE

Your Church. Would you like to make a church like the one on this page? Perhaps you could change it enough to make it look like your church. You must be sure to fold your paper so that the edges fit evenly together. Always crease with your finger nail. Make the church windows with your colored crayons. We must do our best work on God's house. Do you know why? You can make other kinds of houses out of the body of the church. See what you can make. Find pictures of houses you like and paste them on the blank page neatly. They will help you to draw houses for your stories.

Your Friends. What a good time everybody is having! Would you like to make a picture of your friends playing? Look at the boy with the balloon and see how to begin. Notice his head and body are just as long as his legs. His arms and legs bend in the middle. His foot shows a tiny little heel. When we make a stick boy first it is easier to put on his clothes to make him look real. The little boy is only partly dressed. What part of the girl must be made solid? How can you tell the church is across the street? What day is coming soon when we will go to church to thank God for all His lovely gifts?

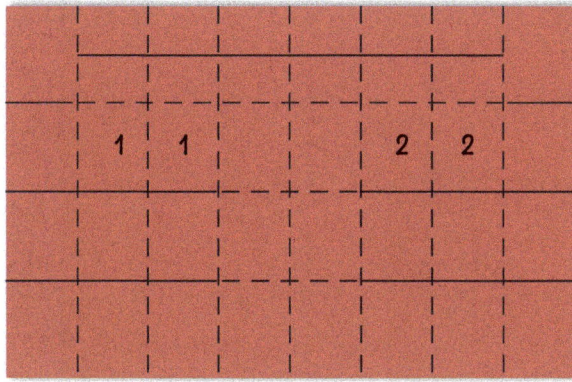

FOLD AND CUT ON HEAVY LINES

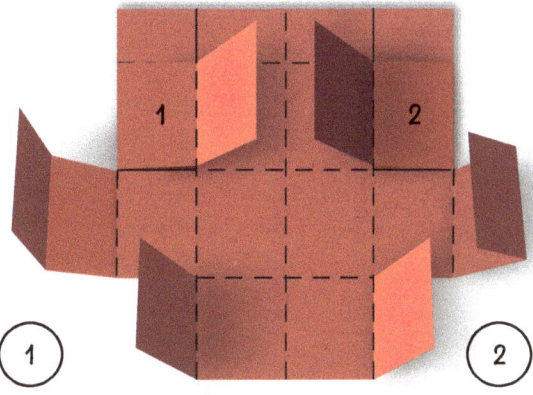

1

2

PASTE 1 ON 1 AND 2 ON 2

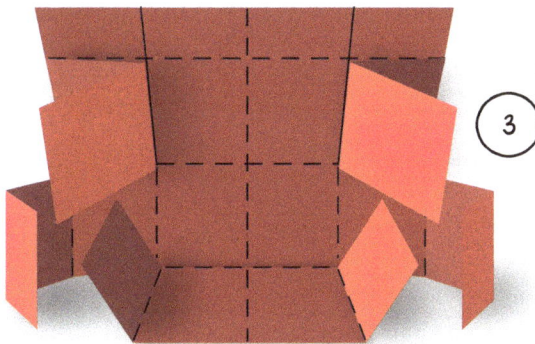

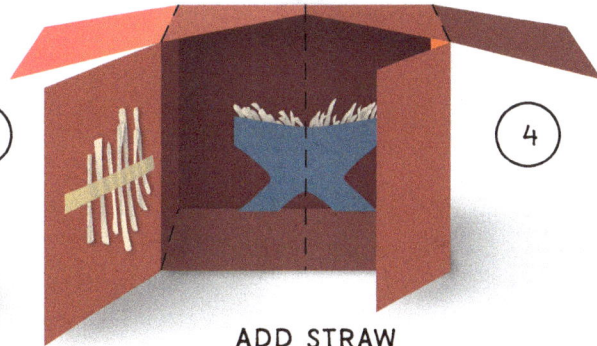

3

4

ADD STRAW

For Baby Jesus. You have heard the story of the stable in Bethlehem where little Jesus was born. Nobody could find room for Him. The animals gave some of their straw to make a bed for Him. They wanted to keep Him warm. Would you like to let Him know how you would have helped Him if you had been there? Look with your best eyes and do just what the picture tells you to do. After your stable is made you can cut the manger shape and paste it. You may begin to fill it with straw. But for each straw you put in His manger you must do some little act to please God. Then God will know how much you love Him.

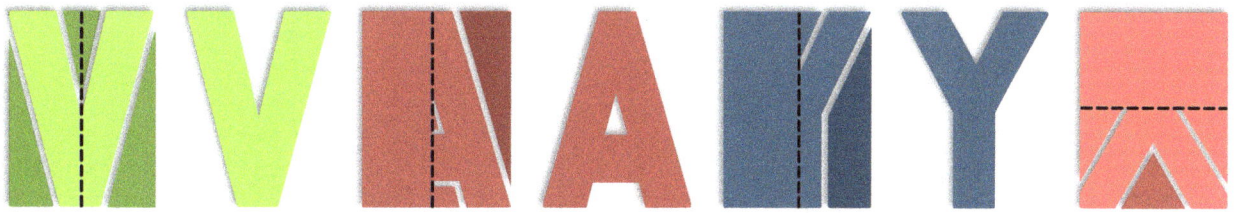

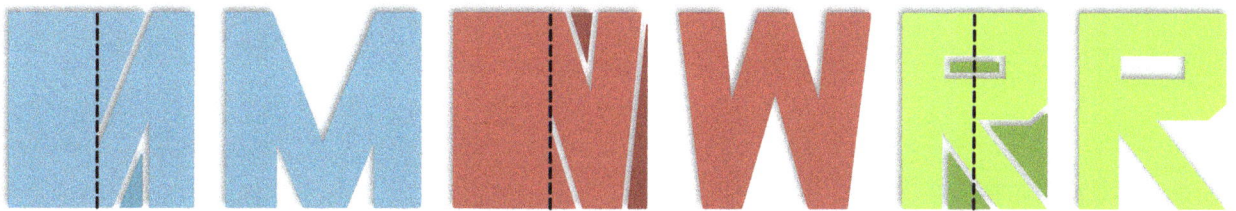

V V A A Y

X N N Z Z K K

M M N W R R

1 2 3 4 5

6 7 8 8 9 0

JESUS

More Letters. Now we have the slant letter family for a visit. We must be very nice to them and learn to know them. Can you find the letters that have two slant parts alike? Which letters have only one slant part? Can you find the only letter in the slant family that has four slant parts? Whose name do the letters make on the page? What do we do when we hear His name?

The First Journey. Did you ever see a donkey? How proud this donkey looks! Do you know why he is so proud? Can you guess Who he is carrying on his back? St. Joseph had to take the Holy Family away to save them. Your teacher will tell you why. You can draw a donkey if you do what the pictures tell you to do. Now try to draw one on the blackboard. See how to make his legs walk. Try making the stick boys. Make them walk and run. Be sure to dress them. That will make them solid like you so you cannot see through them. When you are sure you know how the donkey looks you can cut from paper the story of Baby Jesus' first journey.

1.

2.
PLACE ONE PIECE
OVER THE OTHER

3.
FOLD ENDS OVER.

4.
SLIP ONE WITHIN
THE OTHER.

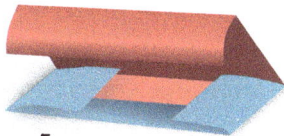

5.

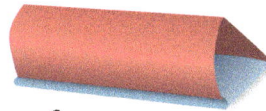

6.

7.
MAKE TWO
DOUBLE OBLONGS.

8.
SLIDE PAPER STRIPS
THROUGH BOTH OBLONGS
FOR THE SIDES

9.

10.

11.

12.

Where Jesus Lived. When Our Lord was a little boy He was poor. St. Joseph was a carpenter. Jesus helped His father just like other little boys do. Sometimes they put pieces of wood together to make chairs and tables. Would you like to play that you were there, helping to make things for our Blessed Mother's house? Can you do just what the pictures tell you? Try to do each step as far as number 7. You can turn the double oblong into a chair or table or something nobody thought about but you. You do not need paste to hold your furniture together. You can use a paper box for your house. Perhaps if you cut out windows you would like pretty paper curtains on them.

Another Party. And this time we are going to act just like big people while we wait to be served. Our little friends are going to serve us. We must be sure to be polite and say "Thank you". What are they serving us? A nice big slice of soft clay. Let us make the bird. Take a small piece of clay. Roll it to look like an egg. Put a tiny round piece on the large end for the head. Smooth with your thumb the place where they meet. When you do this you are WELDING the parts. Now the head cannot come off. Pinch out the little bill with your fingers. God made the world out of clay and water.

LEARNING TO SEE

Can You Do This? Here is a brand new game. Michael and Winnie are showing you how to play it. You must look with your very best eyes. Make sure that you will know which is the top and which is the bottom of the basket. It is wide at the top and not wide at the bottom. This is how you play the game. The girls and boys each choose a leader. Your teacher makes a picture of the basket on the blackboard. The girl leader must hold her basket so that everybody will see that it looks like its picture. The boy leader tries to make his basket look like the new picture your teacher makes. When your leader fails you choose a new one. See who has the sharpest eyes.

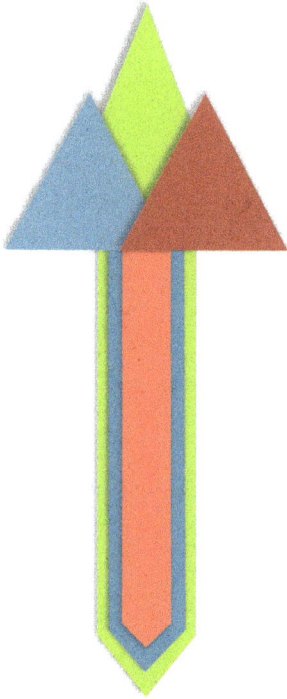

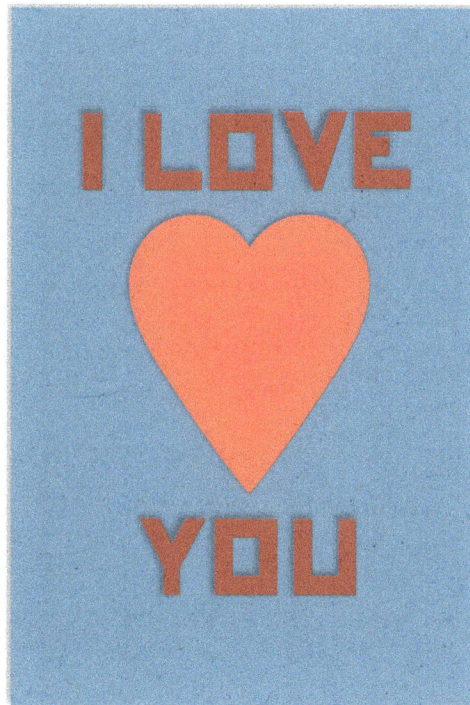

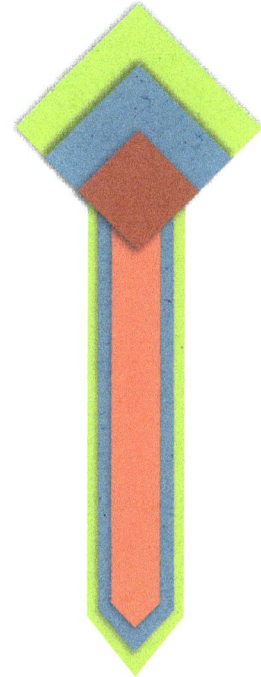

Your Valentine. Did you ever send a valentine? Give your mother a big, big surprise. Send her a valentine you have made all by yourself. It will tell her you love her better than anybody else in the world except your father. Of course, you will send him a valentine too. Fold the paper for the heart. Be sure to hold it shut with your fingers. Cut on the folded side. When you know how to cut a heart you can think of a new way to make a valentine. You send a valentine on St. Valentine's birthday because when he was alive he liked to tell people about the loving heart God has for everybody. That is why we send pictures of hearts to somebody we love.

1. PLACE ONE PIECE UPON ANOTHER.

2. FOLD OVER THE ENDS.

3. FIT ONE WITHIN THE OTHER.

4. FOLD OVER AND FIT INSIDE FOR BOTTOM OF THE BASKET.

5. FOLD IN HALF FOR THE SIDES AND HANDLE.

6. FOLD AGAIN AND CUT.

7. FIT THE SIDES INTO THE BOTTOM AND COMPLETE THE BASKET.

8.

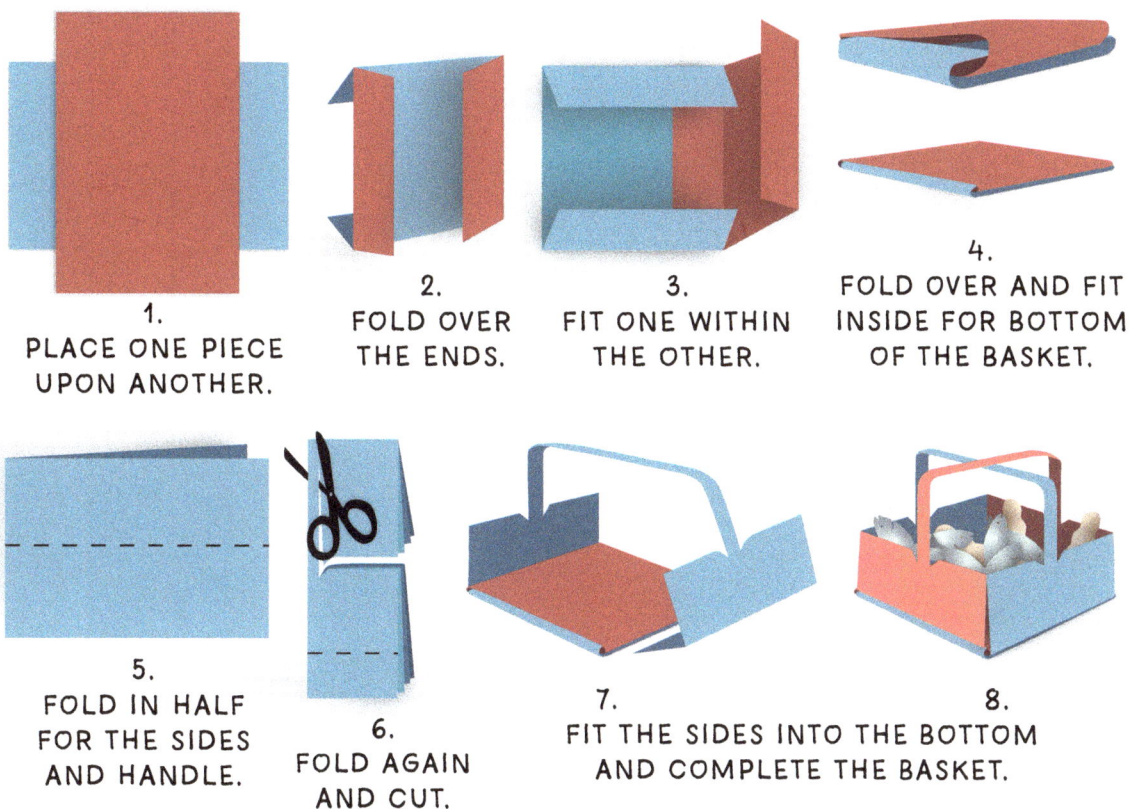

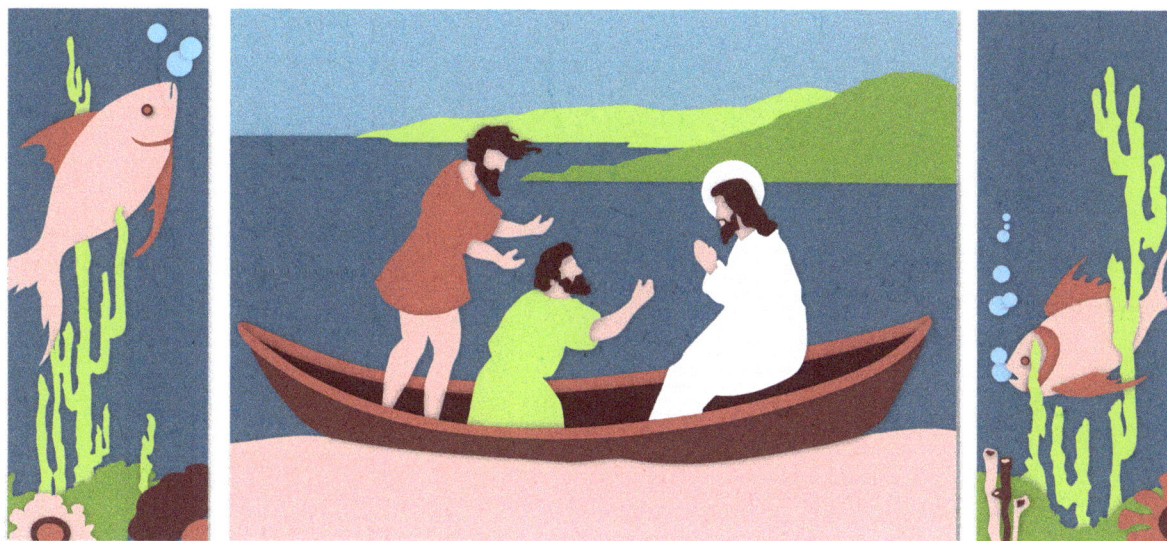

The Little Fishes. Here is Our Lord with His fishermen friends beside the sea. Your teacher will tell you what they are talking about. Make a basket to hold their fish. Begin by making the double oblong you made for your furniture. Number 6 shows you how to cut the sides and handles for your basket. If you wish you may color it with your crayons. Cut each little fish as well as you can. God will know you are doing your best work when you make a picture that tells about Him. The little fishes came into the nets when Our Lord called them. They wanted to show obedience. See what the little fishes are doing on the inside cover of your book.

The Deluge. Have you heard the story about Noe? Your teacher will tell you why he built the big house-boat which he called the Ark. Look inside the cover of your book. You can see some of the animals in the Ark. The dog has his nose outside so that your teacher will see him. He wants her to tell you a story about him. She may tell you stories about some of the other animals some day. Fold a square of paper into four blocks. Then look at the picture and cut the camel by making the scissors follow the path the black line shows. Find pictures of other animals to paste on the blank page. See how many animals you can learn to draw and cut. God wants us to be kind to His animals.

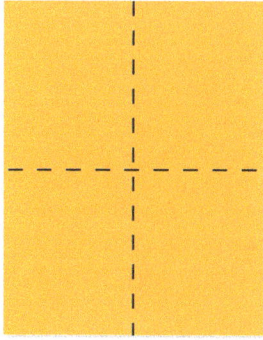

THUMB MAKES PATTERN
ON STEM OF CHALICE.

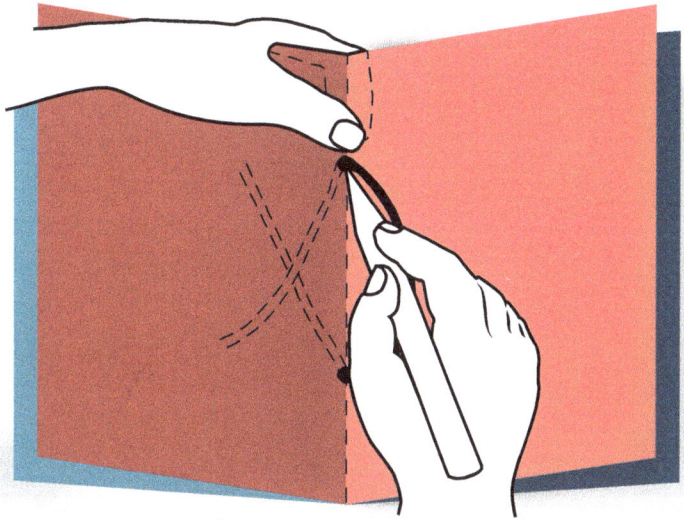

FOLD SHORT ENDS
OF PAPER TOGETHER.
PLACE ONE SHEET
WITHIN THE OTHER.

MAKE HOLES WITH
PENCIL. DRAW
CORD THROUGH
HOLES AND TIE.

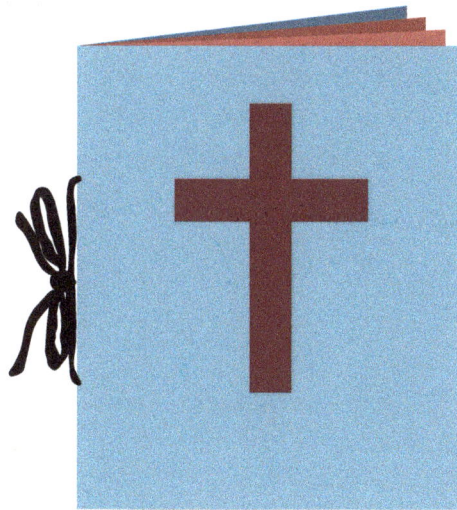

Your Book. Would you like to make a book to tell about being at Mass? Do you remember when the priest opened the little door on the altar? He took out the beautiful gold Chalice that holds Our Lord. Let us try to cut the shape of the lovely Chalice. Fold the paper by putting two short edges together. Open. Fold long edges together. Place your thumb where the lines cross. Cut around it. Make the holes to fasten the pages of your book. Keep one finger back of the book to stop the pencil when it goes through the paper. Color the Chalice like gold and paste it in your book.

PENTECOST

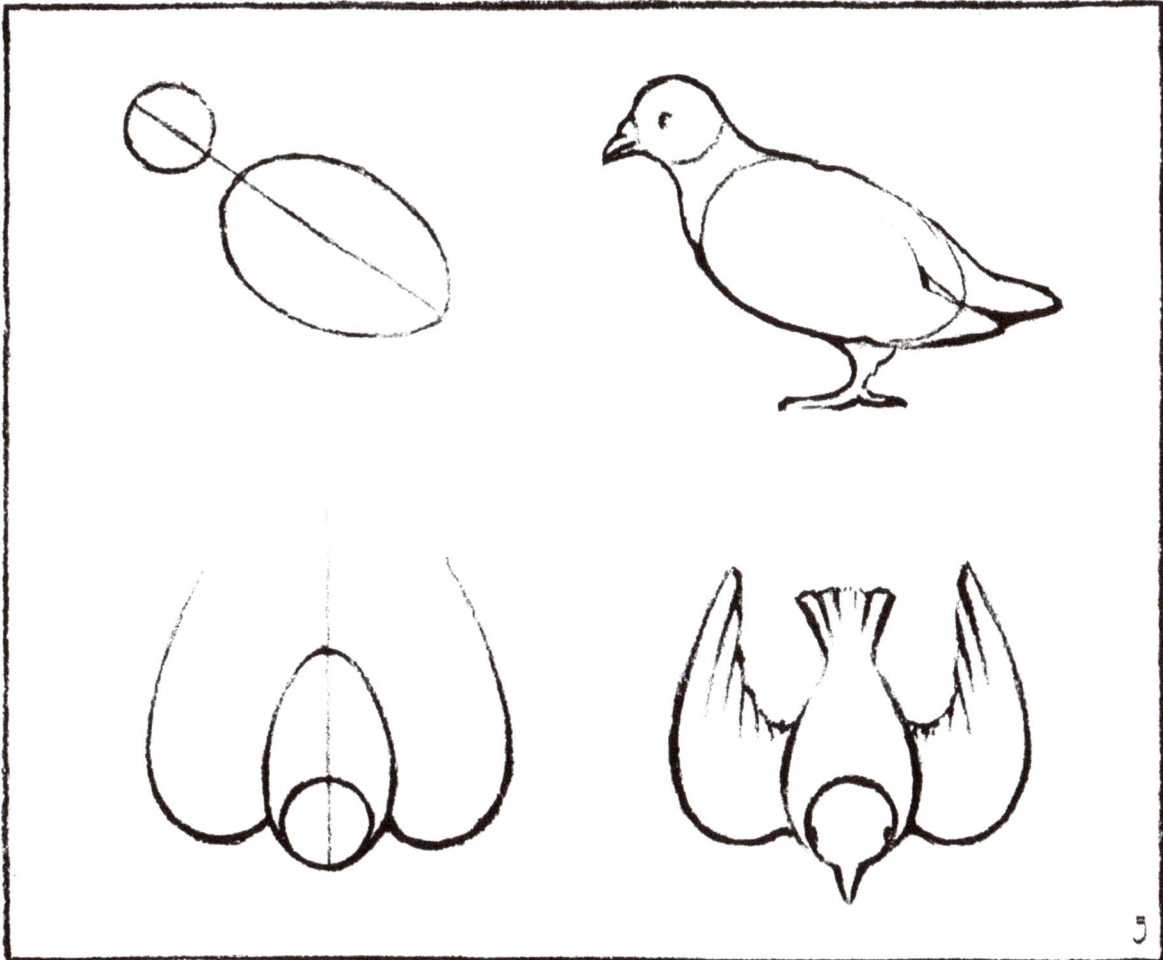

The Holy Ghost. Your teacher has told you about the Blessed Trinity. God is Three Divine Persons, Father, Son, and Holy Ghost, but only One God. When you shared the sunbeams' secret you saw how one sunbeam passed through the glass and became three different colors. You could still see only one sunbeam on the other side of the glass. The Blessed Trinity is God's Secret. Much more beautiful than the sunbeams' secret. We must wait until we go to heaven to have God share it with us. But we know it is true. Ask your teacher to tell you what the colors say to you about each Person of the Blessed Trinity. The dove is the sign of the Holy Ghost.

God's Rainbow. Have you heard the story of the first rainbow? Ask your teacher to tell you about it. Cut from paper the Ark of Noe on the mountain top with the water all around it. With your colored crayons make a picture of the most beautiful rainbow you have seen. Do you know when to look for a rainbow? Do you know how God makes one? The little raindrops up in the sky capture the colors from the sunbeam just like the glass did when you shared the sunbeam's secret. Can you find the rainbow colors on your color page? Can you name them? Do you know where else you may find the rainbow colors? Keep your eyes bright when you see somebody using a hose. Look for one when you see a waterfall. Sometimes you may find a rainbow there. A little Indian boy named Hiawatha heard a nice story from his grandmother. It was about a rainbow. Ask your teacher to tell it to you.

NOTE: FIND PICTURES OF BIRDS TO PASTE ON BLANK PAGE.

SAFETY

Be Careful. Do you watch the lights on the corner before you cross the street? When the light is red you must stand still. The three little children across the street are standing still to let the automobile pass. With your colored crayon make the light tell them to stand still. Make the near light the right color to keep the boy and his sister from crossing in front of the automobile. What color is the light they are looking at? The red light helps your Guardian Angel to keep you safe. You may use your crayons and dress the children in the colors you like. What color shall you use for trees and sky? Hold your crayon like chalk and use the side.

NOTE: FIND PICTURES OF AUTOMOBILES AND CHILDREN TO PASTE ON BLANK PAGE.

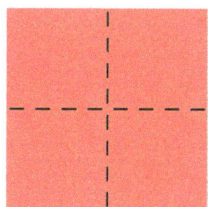

1.
FOLD SQUARE
IN FOUR PARTS.

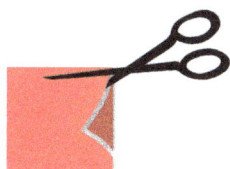

2.
CUT ON THE
OPEN SIDES.

3.
UNFOLD.

4.
CRAYON THE
CENTERS.

MARY OUR MOTHER

Our Blessed Mother. This is the Blessed Virgin's month. God sends us His loveliest flowers to honor His Own Dear Mother. Let us make a beautiful poster to tell people that God loves us enough to share His Mother with us. He allows us to call her Our Mother. Every boy and girl can make something for our poster. Some may choose to cut the letters. Some may choose to cut the flowers. We may ask our teacher if we are not sure just where to place our offering. Our Blessed Mother must have the finest poster we can make. When you make the vase of flowers try to change the shape by a different cut on sides or top.

NOTE: FIND PICTURES OF FLOWERS TO PASTE ON BLANK PAGE.

C IS FOR COLD IN THE STABLE SO DIM

H IS FOR HOME WHICH THE OXEN GAVE HIM

ANGEL'S CROWN

BEARD FOR SAINT JOSEPH

BOOK

BO PEEP

ANGEL'S WINGS

Your Christmas Play. Have you ever been in a real play before? We are going to have one for Christmas. We can make all the things we need for our play. Everybody may help. First we must choose a Director. He will help to make our plans. Let us look at the picture on the next page. What shall we need to make? We must cut the letters for our books. Measure the paper around an angel's head before cutting the crown. After you cut the beard for St. Joseph squeeze it into a ball between your hands. Then smooth it out. Use a flagstick for the shepherd's staff. Use paper rolled on a pencil for the turned part.

The Dream. Do you like the name of your play? The little girl has fallen asleep. The books at her feet are Boy Blue and Bo-Peep. She dreamed the books became larger and larger and then Boy Blue and Bo-Peep came out to talk to her. They told her that little girls should be careful of books. Boy Blue said the book was his house. Every time the little girl dropped it he thought that his house was falling down. Bo-Peep said that the book was her house too. She said that sometimes the little girl forgot to shut it. Then all the dust came in. While they were talking a curtain was taken away. She dreamed she saw what you are seeing in the picture. Boy Blue and Bo-Peep will tell the rest of the story when we have the play. We must always do our very best if we want God to know we like to do His work. God knows everything we do. He wants us to love Him.

www.ingramcontent.com/pod-product-compliance
Lightning Source LLC
LaVergne TN
LVHW070839080426

835511LV00025B/3489